Copyright (c) 2023 Ri4C.

All rights reserved. All photos Ri4C or otherwise fair use or public domain.

This book is sold subject to the condition that it shall not, by way of trade or otherwise, be lent, resold, hired out, or otherwise circulated without the publisher's prior written consent in any form of binding or cover other than that in which it is published and without similar condition including this condition being im-posed on the subsequent purchaser. No part of this book may be reproduced or transmitted in any form or by any means, electronic or mechanical, including photocopying, recording, or by any information storage and retrieval system, without express written permission from the publisher.

Book homepage: Ri4C.com/**TC1**

Dedication

> *Not only has Nick been instrumental in my personal growth, but my family has also played a significant role in shaping me. From nurturing a stronger connection with my mother and enjoying cherished moments of baking with my sister, to engaging in philosophical discussions with my father – I dedicate this book to them, my beloved family.*
>
> *— Edgar "Seadragon" Castro*

Foreword

By Mr. Patrick Boisclair,

Teacher, World History,

Classical High School

> *" Thumoslang, with its roots in Thumos philosophy, intrigues many.*

It is a distinct honor to welcome you, the esteemed reader to another installment of the Raising Seadragon Saga!

This compelling journey full of insights and reflections is a wonderful introduction to and/or continuance of one's Thumos journey and all readers may delight in finding new knowledge in the following pages.

Based on a philosophical standpoint of genuinity and inclusion, the ThumosCode discusses the nature of deep connections and relationships in a world consumed and isolated by technology. Overcoming vulnerabilities, self doubts, and the perils of secondary school, Seadragon pens an articulate vision of what many young people see, hear and feel in their lives across the world.

Acknowledging the reality that "loneliness has reached epidemic levels," Seadragon weaves a personal story of growth, empowerment, and self discovery which speaks through the pages and directly into the soul of the reader. Anyone interested in learning more effective communication and connection strategies could benefit from learning from Seadragon's experiences and lessons about the use of Thumoslang in one's life.

A true coming of age journey with wisdom of the ancestors, imbued with the hope and thirst for new knowledge of the future generations

The Raising Seadragon Saga awes and inspires readers who are willing to suspend their preconceived notions and allow the The Thumos wisdom of the author to guide their personal meditative reflections.

Now is your opportunity to discover a new perspective through the ThumosCode. Are you ready?

Preface

In the intricate tapestry of human relationships that span across nations, there emerges a nuance that is both interesting and pivotal: prosperity does not necessarily translate into benevolence. Instances abound where citizens of affluent nations, despite their wealth, do not embody mutual respect and compassion. Wealth, therefore, isn't the sole yardstick of societal progress; there must be a focus on humanity as well.

Against this backdrop, the vision of an evolved human state—dubbed "Humanity 2.0"—seemed distant and abstract until 2017. It was in this year that the original Thumos textbook was introduced, serving as a beacon, illuminating tangible pathways bridging our present state and our potential future. This is where the Seadragon saga, and consequently, the Seadragon Startup Journey, enter the narrative, embodying a beacon of transformation, mentorship, and education that is crucial for our collective journey towards Humanity 2.0.

Education is fundamental to this transformative process. To usher in Humanity 2.0, our educational systems must undergo a seismic shift, a metamorphosis that doesn't just inform but transforms; turning students not just into repositories of knowledge but into 'seadragons.' These individuals, enlightened and empowered through a refined and expansive educational process, become embodiments of the values and principles crucial for the dawn of Humanity 2.0.

This educational transformation is not a solitary process. Mentorship, as evidenced by the Seadragon saga, is integral. Through mentorship, individuals are not left to navigate their transformative journeys alone. They are guided, supported, and empowered through a process that is as collective as it is individual, as shared as it is personal. The saga of Edgar Castro, or Seadragon, and his mentor Nickantony (Miguel) Quach is a testament to the transformative power of mentorship.

However, transformation isn't spontaneous; it is systematic. To become a 'seadragon', individuals must learn to speak Thumoslang. This language, as illustrated in the saga, is not just a set of words and grammar rules; it is a philosophical tool enabling clear, empathetic, and meaningful communication and understanding. Learning Thumoslang is the first step in the systematic journey of becoming a seadragon, a journey that is both inward and outward, personal and collective.

Furthermore, in this systematic journey, individuals are called to form a chosen family, known in the saga as a 'bongo'. This isn't just a group of individuals; it is a collective founded on shared values, mutual respect, and a common vision. Forming a bongo is crucial in the earlier years, laying the groundwork for the relationships and partnerships that will fuel and drive startup businesses and ventures in the future.

Through Edgar's journey, readers are provided with a blueprint, the Seadragon Startup Journey, which serves as a roadmap showing every young mind how to become a seadragon systematically. This isn't just about personal transformation; it is about life, about crafting a life that is not just successful but meaningful, not just prosperous but also contributive, fulfilling the potential and promise not just of the individual but of society at large.

Therefore, "The Thumos Code" is more than a book; it is an invitation, a call to action, a roadmap, and a blueprint. It invites readers to participate in a transformative journey, to embark on a path that leads to personal and collective enlightenment and empowerment. Upon closing its final chapter, readers won't see an end but a beginning—a lifelong adventure of discovery, connection, and contribution, with the tools, knowledge, and insights necessary for navigating life with purpose and joy. This book is not just a chapter in the lives of Edgar and Miguel; it is an open door to a symphony of connection, understanding, and empathy, beckoning all to participate in the dance of humanity.

Contents

Chapter 1	**Any Teenage Involvement?**	1
Chapter 2	**A Narrow Window of Opportunity**	6
Chapter 3	**From Shadows to Spotlight**	11
Chapter 4	**The Relationship Count Video**	13
Chapter 5	**Cracking the Code of Relationships**	16
Chapter 6	**The Start of Something New**	21
Chapter 7	**My Old Relationship Mindset**	29
Chapter 8	**My Thumoslang Moment**	33
Chapter 9	**My Collapse of Meaning**	41
Chapter 10	**The Relationship with My Father**	48
Chapter 11	**Day 227, Seadragon Year One**	52
Chapter 12	**Seadragon Rising Day**	57
Chapter 13	**The Unexpected Paradigm Shift**	59
Chapter 14	**From Shift to Transformation**	65

1 | Any Teenage Involvement?

[1] Have you ever come across a social code? Think about the game "Rock, Paper, Scissors." Across bustling cities, quiet hamlets, and ancient ceremonies, when someone presents one of those familiar hand gestures, it unites us, revealing an age-old connection. There's no need for a long explanation; it's an unspoken understanding. This is what's known as a social code — a shared vibe that goes beyond mere words.

[2] Continuing with the topic of communication, have you ever paid attention to those 'listening cues'? Picture this: you're describing your day to a friend, and they interject with an "uh-huh" or a nod. It's a way of saying, "I'm here, and I'm genuinely listening." Silence might seem like disinterest, but, in a world where we often feel adrift, a mere 'Ah' or 'I see' from a listener becomes an anchor, affirming to the speaker that they are being heard.

[3] Behind the doors of every profession lies a labyrinth of jargon, a secret handshake understood by only those initiated. Imagine sitting at a café next to two lawyers. They say, "The habeas corpus motion they filed? It's void due to res judicata." To someone not in the legal field, it's like a foreign language. But for them, it's a quick way to discuss a person's right to appear in court and the principle against reevaluating a case. Just as intricate are the unwritten rules of social life, especially when diving into the complex realm of teenage

communication. Their constantly evolving vernacular can often feel as perplexing as legal jargon to those outside their age group.

[4] Which brings us to the question, "Any Teenage Involvement?" Teenagers, with their rapidly shifting slang and expressions, are particularly challenging to understand. Enter the "Thumos Code." Think of it not just as a decoder, but a guide to appropriate reactions to these expressions. When a teenager says, "I'm legit drained," the Thumos Code advises you to disengage, recognizing that they're on the brink of exhaustion or mentally checked out. Rather than merely translating slang, the Thumos Code provides insights into the underlying sentiments, steering you towards an appropriate behavioral response.

[5] But why teenagers? The teenage years are a tumultuous time, filled with emotional highs and lows, and a language that's ever-evolving to express these feelings. While adults may struggle to understand, the Thumos Code, with its emphasis on direct communication and actionable insights, proves most effective with this age group.

[6] Thumos Code serves as a protocol for social life. Essentially, a protocol comprises standardized rules or guidelines ensuring specific actions are carried out consistently and reliably, much like the structured procedures in diplomacy or technology. Adhering to such protocols helps mitigate miscommunications and errors. Thus, embracing the Thumos Code can pave the way for harmonious and effective social interactions.

[7] Thumos Code includes Thumoslang, a constructed philosophical language that offers a structured way to express concepts related to social dynamics, personal development, and more. Amidst the complexities of today's world, Thumoslang shines as a beacon of clarity and simplicity. Unlike verbose definitions, Thumoslang is direct. For instance, traditional definitions might elaborate on "Healthy" as "possessing good health" and "Sleep" as a "state

of rest with reduced consciousness." In contrast, Thumoslang's approach is concise, resembling a streamlined dictionary:

- Healthy; that means, *being fully functional*.
- Sleep; that means, *restoring health*.

[8] Picture a typical teenage scene replayed in households across continents. A mother is getting dinner ready, and she notices her son lounging on the couch, clearly tired from a day of activities. She calls out, "Do you want to be completely ready for your game tomorrow?" He looks up, getting the message. She continues, "That means you need to replenish your energy. It's time for bed." With that, the boy heads upstairs, understanding the essence of Thumoslang through his actions.

[9] Thumoslang isn't a mere adaptation; it's the next evolutionary step in how we communicate. It's a bridge of words, especially to teenagers. It condenses intricate concepts, ensuring that the understanding isn't lost but is found in straightforward, actionable insights.

2 | A Narrow Window of Opportunity

[1] Teens, in the age of Snapchat streaks and TikTok trends, remember those row, heart-pounding connections with friends? Those fleeting moments, bright as an Instagram story but just as quickly disappearing? This window for such irreplaceable moments is razor-thin. Every misstep, every misread text, every misunderstood emoji can lead to lost friendships or viral misunderstandings. The unpredictable digital world makes it even more important to seize every genuine opportunity.

[2] Enter the Thumos Code, a contemporary protocol for the social life of the digital age, crafted precisely to navigate this narrow window. However, to many of you, the Thumos Code might seem like a necessary software update—initially annoying and intrusive but eventually vital. Just as game designers hide learning in mechanics or adults turn vegetables into tasty smoothies, the Thumos Code becomes accessible when related to your daily digital experiences.

[3] It's not just another set of rules. Think of the Thumos Code as the algorithm behind the most successful social media platform that is yet to be created. The Thumos Code will have a significant impact on the digital world, helping people communicate more effectively. This impact will be particularly evident in Instagram DMs where individuals often

struggle to find the right words and, at times, even face the risk of being blocked. The Thumos Code will play a crucial role in facilitating communication for them. As parents and mentors delve into its pages, they're reminded of their own dial-up days, creating a bridge to the 5G world of today. It won't be long before community spaces transform into echo chambers filled with Thumos Code success stories, thus revolutionizing interpersonal connections.

[4] At the forefront of this movement is Seadragon, not a popular YouTuber or a Twitch streamer, but a young man navigating the treacherous waters of modern teenage life. Early 2023 saw Seadragon grappling with familiar notifications – the FOMO, the ignored DMs, the unending comparisons. Yet, in him burned the desire to rewire his social life, making his bond with the Thumos Code all the more electrifying.

[5] Seadragon's journey with the Thumos Code is so powerful that you could say it's akin to the main story of a game. "Raising Seadragon" chronicles his first year, focusing primarily on Thumoslang – the code's unique linguistic key. Behind his gamer-like alias, Seadragon embodies each one of us, riding the waves of adolescence, now powered by the Thumos Code's guiding beacon.

[6] As this chapter unfolds, consider it a tutorial for unlocking Seadragon's transformation. Witness firsthand how intentional likes, retweets, and shares in real life lead to stronger connections, avoiding the pitfalls of ghosting or misunderstandings. The Thumos Code, intertwined with examples from Seadragon's life, reveals how you can reimagine your social settings.

[7] Dive deep into his initial DMs gone wrong, where a missed understanding of a friend's vulnerability led to a lost friendship. Or his earlier approach to friendships, swiping

left or right, not realizing the depth behind the profile. It's these early missteps that set the stage for his enlightening journey with the Thumos Code.

[8] You are not just learning about the Thumos Code. You are gearing up for a journey that will teach the mechanics of making genuine connections. By the end of this chapter, the Thumos Code won't just be another update; it'll be your most-used "app," guiding every tweet, post, and snap, making your social journey clearer, closer, and more authentic.

3 | From Shadows to Spotlight

[1] I'm thrilled to present to you "Raising Seadragon," a masterpiece penned by my mentor, affectionately known as Miguel. This book isn't just a collection of words on paper—it's a vivid portrayal of an adolescence journey, navigated under the watchful eye of his mentor.

[2] Seadragon first encountered Miguel when his friend, Wasser, hinted at a job opportunity in the breezy month of February 2023. With Wasser unavailable, his confidant Junior stepped in to facilitate the conversation. What followed was a crisp and insightful interview, after which Miguel peeling back the layers of the adolescent's persona, decided to bring him under his wing.

[3] This book is not your run-of-the-mill teenage narrative. It spotlights the joys and aspirations unique to those formative years, weaving a tale of personal evolution and the profound influence of one's vernacular, particularly when that vernacular is shaped by the author.

[4] I believe the most compelling aspects of this book are the chapters where Seadragon is with Miguel on his first day at work. These pages burst with extraordinary happenings, the details of which I'll coyly keep to myself. After all, the thrill is in the reading!

[5] "Raising Seadragon" is more than a book—it's a roadmap for adolescents seeking a broader grasp of the world through the eyes of Seadragon.

[6] And here's the plot twist: I am Seadragon! My mentor cleverly rearranged the letters of my full name, concocting the unique nickname from this anagrammatical scramble.

Living the Seadragon life,

-Edgar Castro

4 | The Relationship Count Video

[1] Picture a cozy café, its walls having absorbed years of whispered secrets. Friends gather, their eyes captivated not by the usual viral videos, but by a title that piques their curiosity — 'Relationship Count Video.' The murmurs and occasional gasps signal a shared anticipation. They are on the brink of discovering more than just another online trend: they are entering the world of Thumoslang.

[2] Elias, with a childlike gleam of discovery in his eyes, introduces Armando to Nickantony Quach—the unsung philosopher of our age. As Elias and Armando, two souls in search of meaning, hang on to every word from Nick, the atmosphere is palpable. They aren't merely listening; they're absorbing a profound truth: the essence of life is the depth of our relationships.

[3] The narrative shifts as the screen flickers, transitioning to a mundane scene: a man buying bread from an indifferent baker. From the back of the room, a voice challenges, "Is this what we call a relationship?" It's not merely a question—it's a societal critique. Nick interjects, "Not if there's no heart in it." His statement resonates: relationships are more than just transactions; they are about the soulful moments embedded within.

[4] Nick, speaking with the wisdom of a sage, emphasizes that there's a vast difference between simple interaction and genuine connection. This realization can challenge our preconceived beliefs. Seen through the Thumoslang perspective, Armando's large virtual following appears more like a façade than a true connection.

[5] The epiphany dawns on Armando. Those digital acquaintances? They are often mere shadows passing by. True relationships, illuminated by Thumoslang, hold the rarity and value of gold. Thumoslang doesn't command; it enlightens. It serves as a compass in the journey of understanding. As Nick profoundly asserts, to elevate life, one must first truly perceive it.

[6] As their dialogue nears its conclusion, Elias and Armando arrive at a mutual revelation: Thumoslang is more than just discourse—it serves as a guiding star in the intricate labyrinth of human connections. What if this wisdom were integrated into our educational systems? Surely, an evolution in understanding would ensue, wouldn't it?

[7] The screen fades, yet a palpable transformation fills the room. The 'Relationship Count Video' was more than mere digital consumption—it was an awakening. Armed with insights from Thumoslang, they now stand on a new threshold, poised to journey into the heart of authentic human connections.

5 | Cracking the Code of Relationships

[1] Below is the most important portion of the conversation in the three-way meeting captured by the 'Relationship Count Video' introduced in the previous chapter.

[2] "Take a guess," Nick prompts, locking eyes with Armando, challenging him to confront his own perceptions. "How many genuine relationships do you think you have right now?"

[3] Armando hesitates, a touch of pride creeping into his voice, "568? If I count my Instagram followers…"

[4] Elias, unable to hold back, let out a skeptical huff, "Seriously?"

[5] Nick gestures, reminiscent of a seasoned professor taming a room full of eager freshmen. "Hold on. Let's dive into the Thumoslang view of 'relationship' and then rethink."

[6] Setting the tone, Nick shares, "In Thumoslang, a 'relationship' is defined as ongoing relations." This idea got a revamp some months later.

- UPDATED: Relationship; that means, *ongoing and independent relations*.

[7] Observing Armando's reaction, Nick elaborates, "By 'interaction,' we imply purposeful involvement."

[8] Deepening the explanation, he says, "'Involvement' means causing someone to be part of something."

[9] "Let's break this down," Nick suggests.

[10] Nick motions as if piecing together a jigsaw, one he's put together many times before. "For instance, consider our meeting today. I invited you, ensuring your inclusion. That was a deliberate involvement on my part."

[11] "If this involvement centers around a shared purpose," Nick continues, "it becomes a 'relation,' but not yet a 'relationship'."

[12] Drawing from a memory, perhaps, he adds, "Two bus passengers without mutual goals remain strangers. Mere proximity doesn't signify involvement or relation."

[13] "But today, with our shared purpose of exploring new knowledge," Nick stresses, "we've got a relation."

[14] "But sporadic interactions like a shared coffee or nod don't create a relationship. Consistent interactions, like seeing a baker daily, may form an ongoing interaction, but not necessarily a relationship. To develop a relationship," Nick suggests, "you might want to ask her out."

[15] As Armando tries to process this, he begins, "So, you're implying…"

[16] Nick, always anticipating his pupil's next thought, jumps in, "To truly have a relationship with someone, you need multiple ongoing relations with them."

[17] Armando's eyes show his growing understanding of Thumoslang's perspective, while Nick builds on the topic.

[18] "Like, with Elias here, you've got two ongoing relations: one about school chats and the other, your music jams. Together? That's a relationship."

[19] Armando ventures, "So, if there's only one relation…"

[20] "That's called a 'phantom relationship,'" Nick clarifies. "It may feel real, but it lacks depth."

[21] "Simply put," Nick adds, "a single involvement without a shared purpose is merely a service."

[22] "Got it," Armando replies, the lightbulb fully lit.

[23] Nick, ever the mentor, asks, "Now, considering this, how many real, deep relationships do you think you've got?"

[24] Elias smirks, taking a little too much pleasure in seeing Armando rethink his initial bravado.

[25] "Way less," Armando confesses.

[26] Elias, grinning, teases, "Definitely not nearing 500."

[27] Nick adds, "The precise count isn't as crucial as comprehending the nuances of our engagements."

[28] With a newfound realization, Armando estimates, "Perhaps between 0 and 15."

6 | The Start of Something New

[1] As the final bell of seventh grade rang, its echoing chime tangled with laughter and whispers. While the corridors started to empty, dreams of the months ahead filled the air. Yet, hidden beneath excited chatter, I overheard hushed reverence for "Classical" and its formidable entrance exam. Classical High, known throughout the district as the pinnacle of academic excellence, was more than just a school. With a rich history of producing renowned alumni, from successful entrepreneurs to influential artists, its name carried weight. The school's highly qualified educators made it a dream for many aspiring students. My summer haze became punctuated by the looming question: would my journey take me away from those I held dear?

[2] And just like that, summer was upon us—a dance of fleeting TikTok trends and spirited video game battles, shadows playing to the rhythm of the screen glows. But not all shadows were carefree, some held the weight of decisions yet made.

[3] When I arrived at school for the first day, I decided to take my seat in the front, where I would be closely supervised by the teacher as all the other seats were taken. I didn't sit next to anyone as I didn't have a lot of friends in the class, but after a few minutes, I saw a

familiar face come through the door, it was someone that I hadn't had any interaction with since April during the seventh grade, Davon, I was very happy because I missed him on the last two months of school, so we had a lot of catching up to do.

[4] On the first day of school, we sat together at lunch talking about what we did over the summer. We talked about vacations, how most of us just didn't do anything, and how some exercised. It was nice to be able to talk to him after such a long time. Then the month of September was coming to a close.

[5] Feeling that weight, I turned to my study materials. With a fire in my belly and a hint of rebellion, I chose a test prep book that wasn't quite the norm. Though designed for a different school, it was filled with strategies believed to be beneficial for the Classical test. Observing my friends develop their study methods reinforced my choice. As days turned to nights and the test loomed closer, we all sought our own ways to manage the tension.

[6] One day, as the test date loomed ever closer, my friend, Davon, was wanting to experience a haunted house, keep in mind me and Davon have not hung out before this, so I decided to say, "Hey Davon, why don't I take you to a haunted house, there's one near my house, and we can bring Wasser along with us." I sought a break from our preparations. Inspired by the Halloween season, we decided on a haunted house visit. On our way, the conversation naturally drifted back to school and the future. I ventured, "Are you both planning to take the Classical entrance test?" Wasser, ever the enthusiast, shot back with, "Yes, sir!" Davon, in contrast, shrugged and said, "Maybe, but I'm not all that concerned about getting in." Their differing outlooks only added to the whirlwind of emotions I felt about the impending exam.

[7] Another diversion from our study routine was the talk of a new movie that was taking the town by storm. My parents, understanding the weight of the upcoming test but also

the need for relaxation, allowed me to join my friends for an evening at the theater. However, with the reality of tomorrow's challenges looming, I suggested we leave as the end credits began to roll.

[8] Carrying our school bags like badges of honor, my friends and I sprinted to the theater. From the opening scene to the climax, the film held us captive. But as the end credits started their crawl, the weight of tomorrow nudged me to propose an early exit. The stars overhead seemed to silently urge us to rest for what lay ahead.

[9] As dawn broke, the day of the test had arrived. With every step I took toward the majestic entrance of Classical, the weight of the moment settled in, akin to wading through thick, emotional mud. However, the sight of familiar, equally nervous faces provided some relief from my anxiety. Among them was my friend Jean. I inquired, "Jean, why are you here? I thought you had decided not to take the test." Jean replied, "I am; I just want to see if I can pass." With that, we entered together, holding onto the hope of successfully navigating the test and gaining admission to the school.

[10] As I glanced at the test paper, déjà vu enveloped me. Questions whispered memories of past lessons. That old friend, hope, flickered within — had my diligent preparations merely been revisiting old chapters?

[11] A few months later, an envelope stamped with Classical's ornate emblem lay on our dining table. My heart raced, echoing memories of that one blemish from seventh grade. Taking a deep breath, I delicately opened the letter, juggling fear with anticipation.

[12] The acceptance letter, adorned with gold lettering and cool to the touch, gleamed beneath the soft glow of the room. A tidal wave of emotions threatened to spill over — an urge to shout, dance, and share this monumental news. The first person I chose to

confide in was my friend Wasser. "Hey bro, I've just been accepted to Classical!" I exclaimed. "That's fantastic! I haven't received my letter yet, but I'll let you know once I do," Wasser replied.

[13] A few minutes elapsed, and with evident excitement, Wasser conveyed, "I GOT INTO CLASSICAL!!!" I genuinely shared in his joy. Encouraged by this, I decided to message my other friend, Davon. "Hello Davon, did you also receive an acceptance from Classical?" I inquired. "I just received the letter, and unfortunately, I didn't get in," Davon responded. This revelation brought a tinge of sadness, as it dawned on me that this would mark the final year I'd have the chance to spend with Davon, a friend I had made just this year, I had to let go.

[14] The choice was clear but overshadowed by a storm of emotions. Classical promised academic excellence, but it also meant parting ways with dear friends. After nights filled with introspection, I realized: true growth often requires stepping into the unknown.

[15] As I stood at the crossroads of this pivotal year, I found it whimsically poetic to term it "Seadragon Year Minus One." It was the year just before I met the mentor who would christen me with the moniker "Seadragon," symbolizing strength, adaptability, and uniqueness in the face of overwhelming tides. Looking back, this year truly was a prelude to my upcoming metamorphosis.

[16] The choices I made, the challenges I overcame, and the bonds I cherished during this period were instrumental in shaping the Seadragon within me. The essence of the year wasn't merely about tests or decisions. It was about understanding the depths of my own desires, recognizing the strength of my determination, and honing the resilience to navigate uncharted waters. Each experience added layers to my identity, painting strokes of courage, adaptability, and purpose.

[17] As I stepped into the new phase, with the guiding shadow of my mentor soon to enter my life, I recognized that embracing the unknown was crucial. It was in the unknown that I'd find growth. It was in the unfamiliar terrains that the Seadragon would truly come to life, taking me on a journey of self-discovery, steering my path purposefully, even when it meant swimming against the current.

7 | My Old Relationship Mindset

[1] The practice of head shaving, deeply rooted in various cultures, goes beyond being a mere alteration of appearance. Whether observed in military boot camps, sacred religious rituals, or initiation ceremonies, it signifies a profound transformation—from one's former self to a renewed identity. It isn't solely about convenience; rather, it stands as a potent ritual that symbolizes rebirth and unity, analogous to discarding old beliefs for new ones.

[2] Intrigued by the essence of the Thumos code? It extends beyond external changes like a head shave. Delve into the depths by engaging in a conversation about the 'Relationship Count Video' with a like-minded individual. However, don't just listen to Nick—truly absorb his words. When it comes to relationships, a solitary meeting isn't enough to establish a foundation; it's the recurrent and purposeful interactions that achieve this. It's worth noting that the initiation ritual for aspiring practitioners of the Thumos Code involves watching the 'Relationship Count Video,' just for clarification.

[3] Before I adopted the moniker 'Seadragon,' my perspective of the world was starkly binary. Many of us often oversimplify relationships, assuming that brief interactions can forge profound connections. As an example, during my early days, I once gathered the

courage to ask for the number of a person in my class, Robin. Following that, I decided to text him after school, and this marked the commencement of our first text conversation.

[START OF CONVERSATION]

I greeted, "Hey, Robin what are you doing?"

He responded, "Not much, just got back from volleyball. How about you?"

I replied, "Sounds good. I've finished my homework and now I'm just relaxing in bed."

He said, "Oh, nice. Well, I'm going to tackle my homework now. It was nice chatting with you."

I concluded, "Likewise. Have a wonderful night."

[END OF CONVERSATION]

[4] Little did I realize that this would remain our sole text conversation; subsequently, we mostly engaged in occasional iMessage games.

[5] As time went on, I came to comprehend that relationships aren't nurtured through brief greetings, but rather through extensive, heartfelt dialogues. This misperception played out in school, akin to a tree attempting to take root in shallow soil.

[6] Looking back, I would tread a distinct path in the realm of relationships—not due to regret, but due to understanding. It's a lesson learned: not every encounter blossoms into intimacy. In my youthful days, I mistook a crowd for camaraderie. However, a multitude

of faces doesn't guarantee a single genuine connection. Some resonated with my energy, while others simply passed by.

[7] Genuine bonds necessitate more than surface-level pleasantries perceived through rose-colored lenses; they thrive on profound and meaningful exchanges. I once confused nods for friendships; now, I grasp their depth. Even when surrounded by a circle of acquaintances, the echo of solitude persisted. This prompted me to ponder: is it the quality of connections that evades me, or is it an inherent human longing for something more profound?

8 | My Thumoslang Moment

[1] Thumoslang, with its roots in Thumos philosophy, intrigues many. This subset, centered on understanding human relationships, was my next venture. Here's how my journey unfolded.

[2] In a quiet room, Miguel began explaining Thumoslang. Everyone's attention was on him.

[3] "Imagine a tree," Miguel's voice carried a soothing cadence, capturing the attention of everyone present. As he spoke, his hands moved gracefully through the air, sketching invisible lines that seemed to trace the contours of an ethereal tree. The atmosphere was filled with a quiet anticipation, as if the very act of listening could bring this fantastical tree to life.

[4] "The word 'inclusion'," Miguel's voice grew stronger, infusing the air with the weight of significance, "is like the broad base of its trunk." His hands moved down, outlining an invisible shape that symbolized stability and strength. It was as though the concept of inclusion formed the very foundation upon which this magnificent tree stood, supporting everything that would come to be.

[5] "'Involvement'," Miguel continued, his fingers branching out into the air, mimicking the graceful expansion of tree limbs, "are its branches, actions that spread out." Each branch he conjured seemed to carry a story of its own, representing the myriad ways in which people could engage and contribute. The branches symbolized the diverse paths that individuals could take, extending their reach towards greater understanding and connection.

[6] "'Relation'," Miguel's voice softened, mirroring the delicate rustling of leaves in a gentle breeze, "are the leaves, giving purpose and life." His hands fluttered upwards, as if conjuring a cascade of vibrant leaves that shimmered with vitality. These leaves, like relations, embodied the essence of the tree – the intricate connections that nurtured and sustained every aspect of its being.

[7] "And 'relationship'," Miguel's voice crescendoed, radiating warmth and joy, "That's the fruits borne from all of it. Sweet, ongoing, and nourishing." His hands cupped the air, as if cradling the precious fruits that had grown from the collective efforts of inclusion, involvement, and relation. These fruits symbolized the rewards of meaningful connections, offering sustenance for the soul and a promise of enduring satisfaction.

[8] There, in the room, Miguel's tree stood tall, symbolizing the beauty of human interaction. His message left us contemplating the depth of our own relationships.

[9] Miguel then related the metaphor back to Thumoslang's principles. "Think of moments in your life when you felt 'included', or when you've 'involved' others. Reflect on those simple 'relations' that felt purposeful, and the deeper 'relationships' that stemmed from them."

[10] "Inclusion," he began thoughtfully, "is the passive state of *being part of something*."

[11] "Involvement," he continued, "is the proactive extension of that, for example, *causing* another person to be *included*."

[12] "Relation," Miguel mused, "is when the activity's purpose is shared by both participants. Otherwise, it's an exchange of services."

[13] "And 'relationship'?" He paused, letting the weight of the word sink in. "It is the culmination of these concepts, the fruitful outcomes and enduring ties we forge over time. It calls for at least two *ongoing and independent relations*."

[14] Growing up, Miguel had glimpsed many European countries on the Vietnamese board game 'Around the World.' This seeded a dream in his young heart to experience life on that distant continent. However, the repercussions of war unexpectedly steered him to Texas, shaping his adolescent years through high school, college, and his early professional life. Though he adapted, a subtle unease shadowed him, which only subsided upon his move to Germany — the place where his son was born. It was there that he was introduced to the concept of 'landlocked sickness,' explaining his deep affinity for the Ocean State. Though English wasn't his native tongue, his extensive experience in software testing and quality assurance endowed his words with precision and depth. Having navigated the challenges of adapting to diverse cultures, Miguel garnered a profound understanding of relationships. His insights weren't just theoretical; they were chiseled from the raw trials and tribulations of life.

[15] Back then, those lessons weren't just theoretical for me. In fact, the vividness of the metaphor mirrored the complexities I faced in my own journey of friendships and connections. Miguel seemed to understand this. One day, he unknowingly chose a familiar place to further elucidate the teachings — the Canal Walk, near the East Side Transit Tunnel.

[16] It had been the beginning of my first high school summer when Miguel led me to a spot on Canal Walk where I spent a portion of my childhood. The cobblestones underfoot, the familiar chirping of the birds, and the gentle splash of water against the bridges had taken me back to days of artistry by the water. My younger self, lost in the world of colors and brushes, often forgetting the world around.

[17] That day, while the beauty of the Canal Walk remained unchanged, my life had been anything but static. Miguel's brow furrowed, his eyes piercing into mine, holding a question he hadn't yet voiced. Every time he looked at me like that, he signaled the onset of another perspective shift.

[18] As I stood there, under the dappled sunlight, I remembered my own past struggles as I cradled a freshly minted copy of "Toothpaste Against Loneliness & Distractions." I was surprised to learn that loneliness has reached epidemic levels. I appreciate the analogy involving toothpaste, illustrating that we don't combat loneliness as if it were a tangible enemy. Here is the first paragraph in Toothpaste's Chapter 3, "Think Language, Not Machine."

Thumoslang is the toothpaste against loneliness, distractions, and poor performance. The suffix -lang should give it away as a language. Users must think of Thumoslang as a language, not a machine, an app, or anything that can automatically do the work for the user.

[19] The title of Toothpaste's Chapter 4, "Stop Looking for Friends," made me ponder, "Why was I always desperate for more friends?" This chapter should enlighten readers, especially those who once thought that friendships alone could ward off loneliness.

- Companionship; that means, *the shared experience.*
- Friendship; that means, *companionship without judgments.*

[20] I remember one particular night when I was amidst a boisterous crowd. Their laughter echoed loudly, yet a void persisted within me. Among them was someone who had claimed to be my friend, but it was this very person who spread a baseless rumor, tearing through my reputation. That evening served as a stark reminder of the so-called friends—the fleeting, superficial ones the chapter had warned about.

[21] During a particularly tumultuous time, I grappled with my academic responsibilities. The allure of these fleeting friendships often took precedence, leading to a growing pile of neglected homework and assignments. This wasn't so much a direct result of my friends' influences but rather my own inability to balance social desires with academic duties. When one of these friends unexpectedly severed ties, I was left reeling, further hampering my motivation. This spiral of procrastination often found me racing against the clock, scrambling to complete assignments at the last possible moment.

[22] Not only was I suffering from my loss, but the rumor that was also spread about me caused the majority of the school to hate me. The only friends I had then were three guys who didn't believe the rumor and stayed by my side because they knew the truth about the situation.

[23] Once, as my tumultuous eighth-grade year drew to a close, I held on to memories of being the happiest person at its onset. But the subsequent events had left their mark, making the summer bittersweet. While the past cast its shadow over some moments, the prospect of a fresh start in a new school that fall gave me hope.

[24] After the whirlwind of the past, I embarked on my high school journey with determination to start anew. The unfamiliar layout of the school initially proved confusing, evoking feelings of loneliness that I hadn't experienced in years. However, as the new year dawned, fate introduced me to Miguel. His presence would eventually transform my high school experience, illuminating my path and reshaping my understanding of relationships.

[25] One significant lesson from this chapter reshaped my perspective on relationships. Reflecting upon my life, I realized that the dissatisfaction I felt wasn't because I took friends for granted but rather due to the scarcity of genuine relationships in my life.

[26] Miguel's teachings on Thumoslang clarified the line between mere companionship and profound relationships. This revelation—my Thumoslang Moment—signaled a transformative understanding of human connections.

9 | My Collapse of Meaning

[1] During my personal growth journey, I had a profound insight. Consider adhering to a certain mindset for years and then realizing it may no longer align with your current beliefs. I had such an experience.

[2] My mentor gave me a task: to articulate my ideals. Here was my answer:

Right now, my goals include earning good grades, maintaining a fit physique, pursuing higher education, and becoming a skilled lawyer. However, I feel there's more to life than these goals alone. It's been tough finding supportive individuals on this journey. For instance, someone once invited me to work out with them. I agreed, but the day before our plan, they unexpectedly blocked me. Since then, it's been a challenge to find a gym partner, and I often exercise alone.

[3] My mentor's feedback caught me off guard:

> *If your primary motive in seeking people is to serve your goals, you're looking for services, not true connections. Such an attitude won't build lasting bonds.*

[4] Services? Was that all I had been pursuing? I realized that while seeking assistance for tasks like homework or workouts is valid, being trapped in a purely service-oriented mindset can be harmful. I couldn't shake off my mentor's words: "services don't foster genuine relationships."

[5] Services are transactions, often one-dimensional and objective. They fulfill a purpose, a need, or a goal. For instance, when we hire someone to fix a leaky faucet, it's a service. Once the task is complete, the transaction concludes, often leaving little room for a deeper connection or continuity.

[6] Relationships, on the other hand, are multifaceted and deep-rooted. They're built on mutual trust, understanding, shared experiences, and emotional connectivity. While services are about immediate needs, relationships are about journeying together, growing, learning, and evolving as individuals and as partners. A relationship goes beyond the initial reason for connection; it creates an ongoing bond that is nurtured over time. It's the difference between asking someone for directions on the street (a service) and traveling with a friend on a road trip (a relationship).

[7] My revelation highlighted an uncomfortable truth. I had been navigating my connections as mere transactions — seeking services. But in doing so, I missed out on the richness and depth of real relationships. It was like savoring the appetizer but missing out on the main course.

[8] My mentor's insights exposed a fundamental flaw in my approach. With this newfound knowledge, I felt my core beliefs had been challenged, prompting a pivotal shift in my viewpoint.

[9] "How should I change my mindset to look for relationships instead of services?" I asked, genuinely eager for guidance.

[10] After a moment of thoughtful silence, my mentor replied, "Instead of answering directly, I want to share something more personal with you. I'll write you a letter. Sometimes, the act of writing allows for deeper reflection and provides a tangible piece of wisdom you can revisit."

[11] With a nod of understanding, I awaited his words, which he chose to convey in the following manner:

Bristol, Day 226, Seadragon Year One

Dear Seadragon,

[1] One of the best ways to change your mindset from seeking services to fostering relationships is shift the focus of your life from "Taking" to "Giving." This shift does not take place without understanding the insight behind the term 'focus.' Steve Jobs emphasized the significance of focus with his famous quote:

> *People think focus means saying yes to the thing you've got to focus on. But that's not what it means at all. It means saying no to the hundred other good ideas that there are.*

[2] This quote underscores the idea that true focus involves prioritization and the ability to reject distractions or less important tasks in order to achieve excellence in the chosen area of concentration. It brings about the following Thumoslang thumbnail definition:

- Focusing; that means, *saying no to all else*.

[3] One of the most effective ways to focus on "Giving," is to stop using the words "me," "myself," and "I," in conversations. "Giving," however, does not mean handing over some cash, passing along some homework advice, or completing a task. These are services; others can offer. Again, services don't make relationships.

[4] I recently had a fascinating encounter with a young boy named Harrison while taking a stroll. Out of the blue, he inquired whether reaching 18 years marks the entry into adulthood. Unlike a service-oriented interaction where the answer would be a straightforward 'yes' or 'no', I engaged him in a deeper conversation. I explained to him that adulthood isn't solely determined by age but rather by the ability to envision and plan for the future. This led to a

bond formed on mutual curiosity and respect, something far more enriching than a mere service. Always a walking dictionary, I offered a distillation of insights by presenting the following two contrasting Thumoslang thumbnail definitions:

- Adulthood; that means, *a deliberate future.*
- Childhood; that means, *not future-oriented.*

[5] I then explained that adulthood was about having a planned future, while childhood was a time of fewer concerns. This caught the attention of both Harrison and his mom. They both asked me several times to repeat the two thumbnails. "Adulthood isn't just about age," I clarified to Harrison. "You could become an adult as soon as you can plan your future, maybe even tomorrow." This opened Harrison's eyes to a world of possibilities. He kept in touch with me ever since. I gave him and his family a paradigm shift, which keeps on giving without me. That was enough for them to want me to be a part of their lives. With them, I never asked, "What's in it for me?"

[6] Similarly, when you and I met the businesswoman at her establishment, my approach was different from typical transactional meetings. Instead of just discussing the task at hand, I listened to her, acknowledging her vulnerabilities, and shared my Thumos wisdom. Even though we had no direct transaction to complete, our interactions were rich with meaning and depth. The foundation was set for a meaningful relationship rather than a mere business transaction.

[7] Compare these interactions with your experience at the gym. The person who blocked you might have been approaching the partnership as a transaction — a simple means to an end. Had you both approached it with the intent to learn from one another, to share experiences, and to mutually benefit beyond just the workout, it could have turned into a genuine relationship.

[8] The biggest answer to your question is in Chapter 5, "Vulnerability," of the original Thumos textbook. I asked you to read this chapter because of your question. You may want to study it again. Ever since 2017, the book presents the following two thumbnail definitions:

- Vulnerability; that means, *uncomfortable exposure*.
- Connection; that means, *acknowledged vulnerability*.

[9] If you want to create a relationship, you need to have a relation, which requires involvement and thus inclusion. However, all is impossible without a connection to begin with. How did I connect to Harrison and the business woman? As soon as I acknowledged their vulnerability and comforted them with my Thumos wisdom, they feel connected to me immediately. As soon as we had a connection, I followed up with as many steps as possible in the sequence of inclusion, involvement, relation, and relationship. I'm not having a relationship with either of them, but we're on the way there.

[10] Are you prepared to shift the perspectives of others? I discovered that expertise in Thumoslang will allow you to do that systematically every time with everyone. That is how you can offer the giving that always gives, even while you're no longer around the recipient. Sincerely yours,

-Miguel

[END OF THE LETTER]

10 | The Relationship with My Father

[1] One evening, raindrops traced paths down the window as our living room transformed into a space of reflection—a familiar setting for conversations with my father that I could never fully anticipate. The soft glow from the lamp washed away the exact words, but the essence of our talk about the dynamic nature of civilization remains.

[2] I remarked, "The persistent progress of civilization has precipitated notable transformations. Some changes have unexpectedly brought benefits, while others have ushered us into unprecedented challenges."

[3] My father responded, "True. Consider hunting. Once a necessity, today it's an antiquated practice for most. The majority now obtain their food without ever participating in the act."

[4] Nostalgically, with thoughts of our ancestors in the back of my mind, I countered, "Exactly. When we leave behind activities like hunting, we lose touch with the raw, tangible satisfaction of directly earning our sustenance."

[5] He nodded thoughtfully, "Modern conveniences, though invaluable, sometimes lull us into passivity. We often forget our intrinsic thirst for challenges and the rewards they bring."

[6] Enthusiastically, I proposed, "Perhaps we can evoke those raw emotions by infusing purpose into daily routines. Imagine a strenuous workout before breakfast, making the meal feel like the spoils of a successful hunt."

[7] My father, with a twinkle of curiosity, shared, "I've encountered this idea in a podcast. Your take on it, however, offers a fresh perspective."

[8] Through our words, a subtle thread emerged – the lament for lost practices like hunting, possibly mirroring the gaps in our relationship. Despite the range of topics, this theme echoed the strongest.

[9] As darkness encroached, shadows stretched across our living room, perhaps emblematic of the unsaid emotions between us. Such profound exchanges were infrequent, leaving me to ponder: did they narrow our emotional gap, or magnify it?

[10] The next intimate conversation unfolded three months later, focusing on personal wellness. The ambiance mirrored our previous talk.

[11] "Hey Dad, I've been looking online for ways to build muscle while losing body fat at the same time. I also want to find ways to lose the maximum amount of body fat without losing muscle. Do you know of any other approaches?"

[12] He reflected, "In my gym days, my focus wasn't so analytical. I leaned more towards cardio, emphasizing endurance. That's why our long walks never tire me out. Maybe, instead of chasing strength, consider an endurance-based approach for both cardio and weightlifting."

[13] I responded gratefully, "That's an angle I hadn't fully considered. Endurance could be the key to sustained gains. Thanks, Dad."

[14] "Always here to help. But remember, while exercise is crucial, never neglect your diet. And speaking of well-being, it's late. Get some rest."

[15] Engaging in a few intimate conversations with my dad each year, whether concerning health or delving into deeper philosophical musings, has imbued me with a sense

of being in sync and a communal feeling of belonging. Yet, it makes me wonder why I've never found this resonant frequency with anyone else under the same roof. These profound discussions are rare with my mom or sister, making me ponder the nature of the bonds we forge and the nuances of relationships right under our roof.

[16] My interactions with my mom always felt more routine, limited to the day-to-day chores and pleasantries. With my sister, there was a distance that had grown over the years, perhaps accentuated by our age gap or differing interests.

[17] Each morning, the aroma of freshly brewed coffee was a testament to my father's unyielding support. While he was always there physically, emotionally he was a fortress. Yet, as I delved deeper into Thumoslang under Miguel's guidance, I began discerning the difference between mere presence and profound connection.

[18] While evenings with my father were filled with philosophical musings, my conversations with mom were rooted in the present, often revolving around the practicalities of life. My sister and I, on the other hand, seemed to dwell in parallel universes, seldom crossing paths in emotional or intellectual spheres.

[19] Despite this problem with me and my sister, we one time decided to bake a cake, we would usually bake using cake mixes, but this time we wanted to make a cake from scratch. It went pretty badly because we burnt the cake, but we still enjoyed the moment though. Though with my mom, we would usually talk about things affecting our lives and she would usually tell me about her work drama, which I find pretty interesting.

[20] The rift with my sister began in our teenage years, a misunderstanding neither of us addressed, letting it fester. We both liked different music, and watched different shows, and had different hobbies. As for my mom, our relationship had maternal love, yet there was always an unspoken barrier, perhaps stemming from our vastly different worldviews.

[21] Deep down, I yearned for the same depth of connection with them as I had with my father. But over time, I'd come to accept the unique rhythm and melody of each relationship in my life.

[22] Armed with newfound knowledge from Miguel, I stood at a crossroads: should I strive to fortify our bond, or simply accept the familiar terrain of what Thumoslang refers to as phantom relationships?

11 | Day 227, Seadragon Year One

Providence, Day 227, Seadragon Year One

Dear Miguel,

[3] Your letter, dated Day 226 of SY1, was filled with profound insight and gave me a moment of introspection. Thumoslang, the formal vocabulary for social life, has clearly offered you a potent tool for understanding, and more importantly, nurturing human relationships.

[4] The distinction you made between services and relationships was amazing. The principle of shifting from "Taking" to "Giving" is an essential one. True giving, as you've said, isn't about the tangible alone. It's about the value you bring to the human connection.

[5] Steve Jobs' words on focus have been a beacon for many, and you've highlighted an important thing about it. It's indeed not about merely concentrating on what's before us but rather about determining what to let go of. The Thumoslang thumbnail definition, "Focusing; that means, saying no to all else," perfectly accompanies his words.

[6] Your interaction with Harrison was the epitome of what giving, in its truest essence, means. By reframing his understanding of adulthood, you didn't just answer his question but enriched his worldview. The contrasting definitions of adulthood and childhood that you presented underline the maturity of thought rather than the mere passage of time.

[7] The distinction between transaction and connection is important, especially in the modern world where the former often overshadows the latter. I remember our interaction with the businesswoman and realize the depth of the approach you employed. You showed that relationships aren't built by mere transactions but by understanding and addressing the underlying human vulnerabilities.

[8] You spoke of the gym experience, and it reminded me of the many such moments in life where, perhaps, I approached situations with a transactional mindset. Your perspective serves as a reminder that a slight shift in approach can make a monumental difference.

[9] Your emphasis on the interconnectedness of vulnerability and connection resonates deeply. The concept that a connection originates from acknowledging vulnerability offers a fresh perspective. Your journey with Harrison and the businesswoman aptly exemplifies this.

[10] As for the Thumos textbook and Thumoslang, your expertise and the way you've employed it in real-life situations inspire me to delve deeper. Shifting perspectives isn't just about changing viewpoints; it's about enriching lives. Your letter serves as a testament to that.

[11] Thank you, Miguel, for sharing your experiences and wisdom. I'm moved by your words and inspired to foster more meaningful relationships, keeping the essence of Thumoslang close to heart.

Warm regards,

-Seadragon

Pawtucket, Day 235, Seadragon Year One

Dear readers,

[16] I may be somewhat biased, but I believe the Day-227 letter I wrote just over a week ago was excellent. It was in response to my mentor's Day-226 letter, presented at the end of Chapter 9, "My Collapse of Meaning." While the Day-227 letter primarily reviews the content from the Day-226 one, it serves an important purpose.

[17] I regret not specifying earlier how I'd apply that knowledge to my life. However, by sharing the letter in its present form, I assure you that I've responded authentically to my mentor, and I remain true both to myself and to you.

[18] In the remainder of this book, you'll see how I incorporated my mentor's wisdom. Initially, I thought we'd write more, but after today's review, he believed our narrative was complete. The teachings of Thumoslang have not only given me clarity on past events but also confidence as I step into my next chapter — my second year of high school.

[19] After reviewing all the chapters in this book with several others today, my mentor commented, "We hadn't anticipated it, but the narrative has reached a perfect close. Extending this nonfiction piece might not achieve such a fitting conclusion. We let the unfolding events and their truths shape our story, rather than mapping too far ahead."

[20] With the insights I've gained, I've already fostered deeper connections with my immediate family. As I step into my second year of high school next month, I'm confident that my social life will flourish in new ways.

[21] For those of you in or around Providence, Rhode Island, consider seeking my mentor directly instead of reading his books. The impact he had on my life in just a few weeks was profound — a time frame shorter than it might take to fully grasp the insights from his writings.

Warm regards,

-Seadragon

12 | Seadragon Rising Day

Bristol, Day 229, Seadragon Year One

Dear Seadragon,

[3] Thank you, Seadragon, for meeting with me, Alec, and Steax at Pho Horn's Restaurant yesterday. Not only did Steax say 'Yes' to our invitation to join as the third person in founding a nonprofit for Thumoslang, but he also agreed to meet with us weekly starting from the following week. Yesterday (SY1Day228) was a significant victory for Thumoslang.

[4] During the meeting, at my request, Alec looked into your eyes as he promised you that he would publish the first book, 'Raising Seadragon,' before the next morning. Yesterday was also a remarkable achievement for the Raising Seadragon Saga (**RSS**). As this very book is rapidly becoming the fourth installment, the collection is no longer a trilogy; it's a saga.

13 | The Unexpected Paradigm Shift

[1] Warm light filtered through the café's large windows, casting a cozy golden hue over the rustic wooden tables and exposing brick walls. The soft hum of conversations and the aroma of fresh coffee enveloped the space. By the corner, a barista meticulously crafted a latte, the steam from the machine slightly fogging the nearby window.

[2] "In what way do you intend to apply the insights I shared in my recent letter to you?" Miguel asked, their conversation taking place as they found their seats beside the café's front glass wall, accompanied by an array of plants. The only available table provided the setting for their discussion, where their drinks rested. Miguel's gaze, deep and benevolent, emanated from his dark eyes, while his hair, touched with silver, subtly revealed the passage of time.

[3] Seadragon pondered for a moment, absentmindedly tracing the rim of his cup. "While utilizing the knowledge outlined in the letter might pose some challenges… uncovering someone's vulnerabilities will likely be a challenging endeavor for me." Seadragon's young face was earnest, a contrast to Miguel's maturity.

[4] Miguel tilted his head. Next to him, his trusty backpack rested on the floor, tucked between his chair and a pot of green, leafy plants. "When was the last time you saw someone in a vulnerable situation?"

[5] "At one point, I had a friend who was experiencing bullying...," Seadragon recalled, a touch of sadness in his eyes. "I noticed their vulnerability to such behavior, and they mentioned having the confidence to fight back but refrained due to concerns about their record being tarnished," Seadragon went on. "Consequently, they were apprehensive about the future. I struggled to find ways to comfort someone in such a situation, a challenge that continues to perplex me."

[6] Miguel nodded thoughtfully. "Making a connection and acknowledging vulnerability do not necessarily require a solution." He was thinking of the following Thumoslang thumbnail definitions:

- Vulnerability; that means, *uncomfortable exposure.*
- Acknowledgment; that means, *responding without affirmation or opposition.*
- Connection; that means, *acknowledged vulnerability.*

[7] Miguel continued, emphasizing his point, "The key factor lies in acknowledging vulnerability; an immediate solution for the vulnerable situation isn't imperative. Offering comfort, even in small ways, can often prove sufficient, with the primary focus placed on fostering that essential connection."

[8] After sipping his drink, Miguel asked, "When did you last encounter that experience?"

[9] "One time, I realized that a friend of mine wasn't exactly being bullied but rather ignored," Seadragon shared. "I reassured him that it's alright and that there will be others who won't ignore him, and who will be happy to engage in conversation."

[10] Miguel raised an eyebrow. "What's his name?"

[11] Seadragon paused. "I don't remember."

[12] "Create one; it doesn't matter, but I need a moniker for easy reference," Miguel suggested.

[13] "Zeus," Seadragon offered.

[14] "How did Zeus react to the comfort you provided?" Miguel probed.

[15] "He was happy and told me that he would continue searching for people who wouldn't ignore him," Seadragon smiled. "Zeus also decided to be my friend as well."

[16] "Was that the first time you met him?"

[17] "No, I knew him, but we weren't friends," Seadragon replied, shaking his head.

[18] Miguel leaned in slightly. "Was this the first time the two of you connected?"

[19] "Yes."

[20] Miguel clarified, "Did you have any control over when that connection took place?"

[21] "What do you mean?" asked Seadragon.

[22] "Did you decide that was the moment you could connect with him?" asked Miguel.

[23] "Yeah, I observed how they were treating him and decided to find out what was going on," Seadragon admitted.

[24] "Excuse me for a moment, Miguel," Seadragon said, rising slightly from his chair. "I just need a quick break." He motioned towards the restroom.

[25] Miguel nodded, "Of course."

[26] After a brief pause, Seadragon returned, settling back into his chair.

[27] "You decided to establish the connection, not when he experienced the moment of vulnerability," said Miguel. "One cannot choose the timing of connection; it can only be chosen, or not, when vulnerability arises. Were you aware of that?"

[28] "No, it's shocking," said Seadragon.

[29] Miguel grinned. "That was a Thumoslang moment. Care to elaborate?"

[30] Seadragon sighed, reflecting on his realization. "I used to think that you could comfort someone at any time, but you can truly comfort someone only when vulnerability is present."

[31] "Could you elaborate more on camera? I want to capture your thoughts during this Thumoslang moment," Miguel asked.

[32] "What truly surprised me was the realization that if I aim to connect with someone, it needs to be during their moment of vulnerability," Seadragon spoke into his mentor's recording device. "I don't have the luxury of choosing a later time to approach and comfort them; it must happen when they're feeling vulnerable. This insight was enlightening for me. I believe my previous difficulties in connecting with some individuals stemmed from my reluctance to intervene at critical moments. I hesitated because I disliked intruding. Consequently, when I tried to reach out later, they often didn't want to discuss the matter. Now I understand that to truly connect with someone, I must be present and offer comfort during their moments of vulnerability. This revelation is profound for me."

[33] Miguel pressed, "Do you begin to understand why people struggle to connect?"

[34] "Yes, I now understand why," Seadragon acknowledged.

[35] "Why do you think Chapter 2 [of this very book] carries its title as 'A Narrow Window of Opportunity?'" asked Miguel.

[36] "The chapter is titled as such because you can only connect with someone when their vulnerability is present," Seadragon answered, his voice filled with newfound understanding. "After that point, you no longer have the choice to decide when you wish to establish a connection. This limitation creates a narrow window of opportunity."

14 | From Shift to Transformation

[1] "When was the last time you had a connection with your mom?" Miguel inquired, his brows furrowed in concern.

[2] Seadragon hesitated for a moment, "Based on the thumbnail definition of connection, I've never had one with my mom. Sometimes she would argue with her brothers, but I stayed out of it because it felt embarrassing. I would wait until afterward."

[3] Miguel leaned forward, his expression thoughtful. "No wonder she has a hard time saying yes to all that you want to do with or for your life. Based on my experience, she'd be more in sync with your wishes if you two had a genuine bond, the kind Thumoslang describes."

[4] Realization flickered in Seadragon's eyes. "You've done it again," he sighed. "You've shown me another thing I need to work on in my life. I'll try harder to bridge that gap with my mom."

[5] Miguel's face brightened, "Got your earbuds handy?"

[6] Rummaging in his pockets, Seadragon pulled them out, "Yeah, here they are."

[7] After sending a link to the video [Video Letter to Lucia | NDBaker93 | S3E1] (v= fvWXY4RRMfI), Miguel urged, "Watch this video. It's about Jairson's journey, another Thumoslang learner."

[START OF THE LAST PORTION OF THE VIDEO]

[8] "Thumoslang has been instrumental in helping me heal my relationship with my mother," said Jairson. "We were at odds for a while, and now I realize that our ideas were in different places. I didn't understand what she wanted from her life, which prevented me from connecting properly with her. Instead, I was primarily focusing on my own desires and occasionally sharing updates about my life, regardless of whether she would receive the information well or not. This approach caused a lot of tension between us because I am currently in a stage of life where I'm developing and pursuing various projects."

[9] "Each time I embarked on a new project and later decided it wasn't suitable for me, she saw it as a waste of time since I wasn't taking steps to secure my future," Jairson continued. "My previous behavior involved not being entirely honest with her; I only revealed what she wanted to hear so I could continue acting independently. I've now come to understand that her frustration stemmed not from my desire to pursue my interests, but from my tendency to do so alone. I've realized that to genuinely love and connect with her, I need to acknowledge that she wants to be a part of my life's journey and that I'm actively and thoughtfully working towards a better future."

[10] "While things still occasionally feel uncertain, they have greatly improved recently because I now understand her desires," said Jairson. "I can now demonstrate how my

actions align with her wishes, proving that my endeavors are not a waste of time for either of us. This newfound understanding has helped us move closer together than ever before."

[11] "In delving into the vocabulary of Thumoslang, what I did, what I'm currently doing, and what I've just discussed is that I took the initiative to learn about my mother's "business-of-the-self," said Jairson. "Through this, I gained insight into the aspects of her envisioned future that I was previously unaware of. Subsequently, I was introduced the concept of respect, which emphasizes non-interference. It entails stepping back and aiding someone in their pursuit of ideals and goals. Previously, my lack of knowledge about my mother's ideals hindered my ability to respect them. However, now that I've come to understand them, I've begun to respect them, and this has played a significant role in bringing us closer together."

[END OF THE LAST PORTION OF THE VIDEO]

[12] Seadragon shook his head in disbelief, "It's incredible that someone had the same problem as me. Watching this video was an eye-opener."

[13] "So, what's your plan?" Miguel pressed, eyes piercing into Seadragon's. "What's the first real step you'll take?"

[14] Seadragon shifted in his seat, "Before I answer that, can I quickly go to the restroom?"

[15] Miguel nodded, "Sure, take your time."

[16] After Seadragon returns:

[17] Looking uncertain, Seadragon admitted, "I don't have a step-by-step process; I just hope to seize the moment when it comes."

[18] Miguel cocked an eyebrow, "And how will you ensure that moment comes?"

[19] Rubbing his chin, Seadragon speculated, "Observing her during vulnerable moments, like those arguments with her brothers, might be a chance to connect. But it's hard to plan these things. They just happen."

[20] "You can't force vulnerability," Miguel agreed, "but you can be ready for it. How?"

[21] Drawing a deep breath, Seadragon said, "Connecting with my mom means gathering courage and determination. If she stumbles or feels embarrassed, I should be there to offer a comforting word or gesture."

[22] Miguel frowned, "You're evading my question."

[23] "Alright, alright," Seadragon conceded. "To truly connect with her, I need to be present during her moments of vulnerability."

[24] Miguel nodded, "Using abstract verbs isn't helpful. Action, Seadragon. Think action."

[25] Miguel reiterated, "You cannot create the moment of vulnerability, but you can create the opportunity to seize it. How?"

[26] "To actively engage with my mother when she's vulnerable, that's the key," Seadragon declared.

[27] Miguel tilted his head, "What held you back before?"

[28] Avoiding Miguel's gaze, Seadragon murmured, "Embarrassment, mostly. I felt too awkward to approach her during those times."

[29] Miguel observed softly, "Perhaps you also weren't around her enough."

[30] Nodding slowly, Seadragon whispered, "That's right…"

[31] Miguel's voice softened, "You've connected with acquaintances more than once. You do know how to connect. The issue isn't capability. The reason why you didn't with your mother was not because you didn't want to, but you weren't there enough to be a part of her life, hence the lack of opportunities."

[32] Seadragon shifted uncomfortably, "It's hard being there consistently, Miguel. She's so often working, and when she comes home, she's exhausted. If she's up for it, we might chat. But yes, sometimes, I don't engage either. After my own work, I just want solitude."

[33] Miguel leaned in, pressing the point, "If you're not invested in her life, why should she be in yours?"

[34] With a pointed look, Miguel emphasized, "You need to be there, especially when she's drained or feeling low. Those are the moments she might need comfort the most."

[35] Miguel paused, letting his words sink in, "Did you ever think of just bringing her a glass of water when she's tired?"

[36] "It didn't take much to connect, unless you lack Thumos knowledge," said Miguel.

[37] "You're right," said Seadragon. "I should be able to connect with her more now. I didn't realize that tiredness is a moment of vulnerability. Knowing this now, there were so many missed opportunities where I could have connected with her. Understanding this can help me improve my relationship with her."

[38] Miguel gestured for emphasis, "The answer is simple. Stay close. Do your homework near her. Play your games around her. If you're out of sight, you're out of mind."

[39] A hint of surprise in his voice, Seadragon remarked, "I never expected to delve this deep into my family issues with you. This… this means a lot, Miguel. Thank you."

[40] "Anytime, Seadragon." With a warm smile, Miguel concluded, "We've just nailed the meaning of 'Raising Seadragon.'"

[41] In the waning moments before Small Point Café shut its doors on 'Seadragon Rising Day,' Seadragon and his mentor had achieved a profound and unmistakable comprehension of what it truly means to sail through in the process of 'Raising Seadragon.'

The End

The year was 2036, and I was a college sophomore named Casey Dagher, living on my own in Washington, DC. However, my life took an unexpected turn when I was brutally stabbed to death in an alleyway, just days before summer. But that wasn't the end for me. I awoke in a mysterious place, discovering that I had been granted extraordinary abilities; superhuman strength, unparalleled precision, and a mechanical humanoid body. Reborn with power, a secret government program gave me a second chance at life. I'm now known as special agent Jaklyn Lionheart, the alias I assume to conceal my true identity, appearing to be an ordinary-looking person to the world. My mission is to protect innocent people by stopping those who misuse their robotic powers, just like mine.
This is my story.

Loneliness is like decay-causing bacteria. It hurts you over a long period, not within a few hours. As a health risk factor, loneliness is more like obesity and smoking. According to Loneliness and social isolation as risk factors for mortality: a meta-analytic review by Holt-Lunstad, et al., 2015, obesity and smoking lead to the same risk for premature death as loneliness. You cannot kill loneliness once and for all. You cannot fight loneliness with a weapon used in a single battle. To prevent loneliness, think of using toothpaste, not a weapon. You need to work at it as frequently as you brush your teeth. It's that easy, but it takes time and a lot of perseverance. Thumoslang is the toothpaste against loneliness; the following pages offer usage and directions. By eight years of age, children should have a foretaste of Thumoslang. It's never too late to learn Thumoslang, but the earlier, the better.

This book documents the experiences of inner-city school teachers and their lack of support in educating students, attempting to determine the root cause of their struggles. No matter who I am, my teachers never told me I could control my future despite my environment, which I have little control over. My biggest problem at my inner-city school is the lack of training to discharge such power. That's why I have nothing better to do than join my peers and do some non-learning activities mentioned above. Am I supposed to tell my parents about any of the above issues? Calling the parents does not help when the student does not have parents interested in their child's future as much as generally expected by society. Increasing the quality of teachers does not help. Better schools also experience the issues mentioned above, though to a lesser extent.

- Life in 184 Words, aka. Thumoslang on the Run (**OTR**)
    - This book, Life in 184 Words, also known as The Guide to Thumoslang, helps you increase the productivity of your group, advance the progress of your community, and make your own life better. Learn to keep yourself on the shortest path towards your desired life path without needing to put blind faith in parents, religions, or other forces. Using all you learned from them, Thumoslang helps you see what they taught you in a new light.

- Thumoslang for Character Renovation (**TCR**)
    - Using Thumoslang, the author attempts to trace the slow-burn personal transformation of several Thumoslang students. The more you command thumbnail definitions, the more you are fluent in Thumoslang. With this fluency, you can be far more powerful than you have been led to believe. With the science of Thumoslang, people can discover their true capacities through a slow-burn transformation. That is a way to test your power and thereby keep your loneliness at bay for good.

Edgar Castro

In the heart of a world where books are like windows to different realms, Edgar, known among his close circle as "Seadragon," unearthed the privilege to make significant contributions to "Raising Seadragon." This manuscript, a Thumoslang piece crafted by Nickantony "Miguel" Quach, greatly benefited from Seadragon's youthful lens. While the book brimmed with profound insights, the perspective risked alienating its young readers, something Edgar sensed acutely.

This collaborative expedition between Seadragon and Miguel had ripple effects throughout the book. For readers, their partnership is a testament to the power of mentoring and the merging of youthful exuberance with seasoned wisdom.

Nickantony Quach

A resident of Providence, Rhode Island, Nickantony "Nick" Quach enjoys riding a bike around town and meeting people on Thayer Street, a popular destination for students from nearby colleges. This street was where Nickantony taught a 2015 graduate of Brown University the first Thumoslang thumbnail definition ever created; **respect** (on page **65**.) The student used it over the following weeks to effectively wipe out the most recurring, troublesome issues with his parents, as he reported to Nick in an email.

At a city in Texas, 1800 miles away, Nickantony came up with the definition 14 years earlier as the first and only lesson throughout the first grade for his son. He did not intend to use it anywhere else. Until he received the email from his mentee, he did not think much of its potential for widespread effect. Soon after, he nurtured a desire to write about it.

Unexpectedly, less than a year later, Mark Canny met and joined Nickantony with the same desire, but for a much greater cause. In April 2015, the writing began for what would become the book "Thumos: Adulthood, Love, & Collaboration."

Alec Mustafayev

Alec Mustafayev (born 2002) is the second high school student who has ever encountered Thumoslang. Part of this experience is captured in the video, "No Rules", which is Episode 8 in Season 7 of the YouTube series NDBaker93. As a matter of fact, his reaction to Thumoslang is captured by the 20 episodes in Season 7 of NDBaker93.

Alec did not always think of myself as a writer, but had been coming up with creative storytelling ideas for his entire life. By the time he was in his freshman year of highschool, so many of these ideas had added up in my mind over time that Alec felt that needed to put them to use. He self published his first book, **Rebellious**, at the age of 15.

Quach and Mustafayev Group

QMG stands for the Quach & Mustafayev Group, formed in August 2020 by Nickantony Quach (pictured, right) and Alec Mustafayev (left). They and their associates work under the QMG banner. **Scan the QR codes** beneath each of them to learn more about them. QMG is the operator of Ri4CTV, a channel on YouTube. Its sister channel on Instagram goes by the same name. The following pages display their various projects.

Made in the USA
Middletown, DE
29 October 2023